It's Not Fair

Marta doesn't want Noah in her story. She wants her friend Shamika. Ms Fable says they have to take it in turns, but Marta doesn't think that's fair. When Noah becomes upset because of how Marta is behaving, she begins to realise that playing with other children can open up a whole load of fun she had never imagined possible...

This beautifully illustrated story book explores a common situation that arises for children and teachers taking part in Helicopter Stories and allows the children to explore their feelings in a sensitive and supportive environment. The story is accompanied by teacher's notes on how to use the book with young children along with questions and discussion prompts that can be incorporated into the curriculum.

In a class where Helicopter Stories take place regularly, *It's Not Fair* explores friendship and fairness and the value of taking turns. It is part of the *Helicopter Stories Tale* series, a valuable and visually captivating resource for all Early Years educators using storytelling and story acting with their children.

Trisha Lee is a writer, theatre director and storyteller. She was the first to pioneer Helicopter Stories in the UK and she founded the theatre and education company MakeBelieve Arts in 2002.

Amie Taylor is a writer and artist. She founded her shadow puppetry and illustration company 'The Shadow Makers' in 2013 and now delivers workshops and projects in creating shadow work and illustration.

"These picture books bring to life the magic of Storytelling and Story Acting. The authentic examples and quandaries are compelling. Trisha gives advice based on her vast experience but also includes the voice of Vivian Gussin Paley herself. This book will be an invaluable resource for anyone who is developing the art of Helicopter Stories in their setting."

Anna Ephgrave, author of five books around the topic of "Planning in the Moment"

"Childhood deserves to spend its days in an immersive world of story and make-believe, and yet again, Trisha shows us how. The rich possibilities she has created here enable an exploration, not only of Helicopter Stories, but of who we are in the kingdom of play. A true adventure awaits you within its pages.

Holding hands with Trisha's words are the wonderful illustrations of Amie Taylor, that turn up the dial of imagination and invite us in to story dream even more."

Greg Bottrill, author of Can I Go and Play Now – Rethinking the Early Years and School and the Magic of Children

"Trisha Lee has written a lovely, accessible set of stories that can be dramatized through the Vivian Gussin Paley method. It is set in the classroom of Fiona Fable, who knows that every child has a story inside them, and her job is to find a way to let those stories out.

These stories bring to light the importance of children being able to tell their stories right here and right now. It's a beautiful and natural way of allowing children to address their worries, share their ideas and catch a glimpse of their imaginations.

We have used this approach for many years at LEYF [London Early Years Foundation], and it has made us so much more alert to the power of storytelling. Everyone has a story, and this book gives you the tools to make this part of your daily life of any classroom. It tells the teacher to watch very carefully, and you will see the children's stories dancing through the air. It is joyful."

June O'Sullivan, CEO of London Early Years Foundation, and author of numerous publications about the Early Years

It's Not Fair

A Helicopter Stories Tale

TRISHA LEE ILLUSTRATED BY AMIE TAYLOR

Routledge
Taylor & Francis Group
LONDON AND NEW YORK

Cover image: Amie Taylor

First edition published 2023
by Routledge
4 Park Square, Milton Park, Abingdon, Oxon, OX14 4RN

and by Routledge
605 Third Avenue, New York, NY 10158

Routledge is an imprint of the Taylor & Francis Group, an informa business

British Library Cataloguing-in-Publication Data
A catalogue record for this book is available from the British Library

ISBN: 978-1-032-05378-3 (pbk)
ISBN: 978-1-003-19730-0 (ebk)

DOI: 10.4324/9781003197300

Typeset in Antitled
by Apex CoVantage, LLC

For Vivian

IT'S NOT FAIR

A HELICOPTER STORIES TALE

TRISHA LEE

ILLUSTRATED BY AMIE TAYLOR

David Fulton Book

Introduction

Helicopter Stories is based on the work of American kindergarten teacher and author Vivian Gussin Paley. It was pioneered in the UK by Trisha Lee and theatre and education company MakeBelieve Arts.

Helicopter Stories is, in theory, a simple approach; children tell their stories to an adult scribe, who writes their words verbatim on an A5 sheet of paper. These stories are then acted out around a taped out stage.

It's Not Fair is based on a real-life situation in an Early Years classroom. It presents one of the principles of Helicopter Stories - the issue of choosing. I have seen several children struggle with this over the years I have been delivering Helicopter Stories. *It's Not Fair* explores how one child I worked with eventually found joy from including other children in her story.

At the end of the book, you will find more information about the strategies I use when children protest that *It's Not Fair*. You will also find a copy of Marta's story.

It's Not Fair is suitable for children aged 3 to 7.

In Fiona Fable's classroom, if you watch very carefully, you will catch a glimpse of imagination

dancing through the air.

And everyone is friendly, and everything is fair.

Well, it was... **until today.**

"I don't want HIM in my story,"
shouted Marta, stamping her feet.

"I
WANT
SHIMEKA."

"Remember, when we do Helicopter Stories, we take it in turns," said Fiona Fable. "It's Noah's turn to be the puppy. Everyone has a go, that way, it's fair."

Noah crawled onto the stage.

"Woof, woof," he said.

"It's not fair," said Marta. "My puppy doesn't bark like that.

She
GROWLS"

"Grrrrrrr ..."

said Noah,

growling his very best growl.

"It's not fair," said Marta. "My puppy doesn't growl like that. She YAPS."

"Yap,
yap,
yap,
yap,
yap,"

said Noah,
yapping his yappiest yap.

"It's not fair," said Marta. "My puppy doesn't yap like that. I don't want Noah in my story. I want Shimeka. Noah is not my friend."

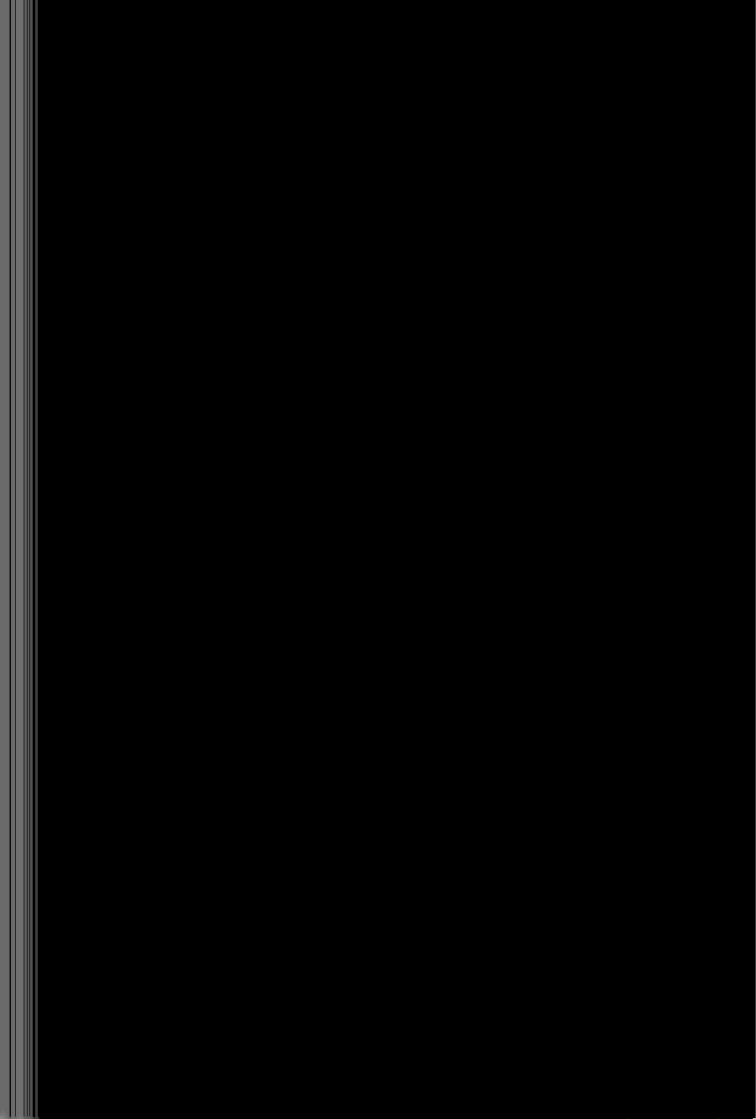

A tear rolled out of his eye and

splashed
onto
the
floor.

It was followed by
another
and
another.

Marta stared at Noah.

Her insides gurgled.

"I'll be your friend,"
said Daisy putting her
arm around Noah.

"Maybe Daisy and Noah could both be puppies in your story," said Fiona Fable.

Marta nodded. She didn't know what else to say.

"Once, there was a little girl, who went into the forest with her two puppies," read Ms Fable. *"A dinosaur chased them."*

Marta watched as Daisy and Noah crawled around the stage, chased by Oliver, the dinosaur.

The dinosaur **roared**.

The puppies **Yelped**.
The children on the stage **giggled**.

Marta longed to join in.

"*Then the dinosaur trapped the girl and the puppies in a cage,*" read Ms Fable.

"Marta, do you want to be the girl trapped in the cage with the puppies?" But Marta shook her head.

"Then a great bear came to save them," read Ms Fable. "Shimeka, will you be the bear?"

Shimeka **shaped her hands into claws.**

"Come on, Marta," said Shimeka. "You be the girl in the cage. Then I can save you." Marta looked at the other children, they all wanted her to join in.

"Go on, Marta," said Daisy.

"**Please**," said Noah.

Marta shuffled inside the pretend cage and gently stroked Noah, the puppy.

"Raaah," growled Shimeka **ripping open the bars**. "I have saved you all."

"Thank you, Mr Bear," said Daisy, slowly crawling out of the cage.

Everyone clapped and Marta
beamed with pride.

"That was a good story," said Noah.

"A very good story," said Daisy.

Marta looked at the children who had helped to bring her story to life.

Children she'd never played with before.

Children who wanted to play with her again.

Maybe it was fair after all.

Teachers Notes - It's Not Fair

"We hold the classroom family together as we demonstrate our curiosity about every dream and story, as we worry along with all who complain and all who cry over every new kind of anguish."

Vivian Gussin Paley – The Boy Who Would Be A Helicopter

Once you have read *It's Not Fair* to your children, think about initiating a conversation with them, using some of the starting points below.

- Why was Marta so cross at the beginning of the story? Have you ever felt like that? What happened?
- How do you think the other children felt seeing Marta so angry?
- Why do you think Noah started crying?
- I wonder what made Marta change her mind in the end and join in the acting out of her story. What do you think?
- Tell me what might have happened to the girl and the puppies in Marta's story if the bear hadn't come to save them?

Ask your children if they would like to act out Marta's story.

Marta's Story

Once there was a little girl who went into the forest with her two puppies. A dinosaur chased them. Then the dinosaur trapped the girl and the puppies in a cage. Then a great bear came to save them. "Raah," said the great bear. "I have saved you all." "Thank you Mr Bear," said the puppy.

When you act out this story, take it in turns around the stage, just like they do in Fiona Fable's classroom. As well as having children playing the roles of the puppies, the dinosaur and the great bear, you might want to invite a few children to be the trees in the forest. You could also ask four or five children to become the cage. Whenever I ask children to pretend to be an inanimate object, I introduce the idea like this:

"1, 2, 3, 4, 5, will you stand up and pretend to be a cage that the puppies and the girl are trapped inside. I wonder how you are going to do this? Can you show me?"

Give the children plenty of time to solve the problem. If they are struggling, ask if any of the other children have an idea for how they might use their bodies to make the cage. You don't need to show the children a correct answer. Whatever they come up with is fine, even if they are just standing still.

Here are some quick pointers to help with the acting out:

- Gather the children in a circle around a rectangular, taped out stage. Alternatively, get children to sit around the edges of your classroom carpet.
- Read the story, one line at a time, inviting individual children to become each character and act out that segment of the story before moving to the next sentence.
- At the end of the story, clap thank you, and everyone sits back down.

For more information on how to deliver Helicopter Stories, read *Princesses, Dragons and Helicopter Stories* by Trisha Lee, which is a how-to on the approach or visit https://helicopterstories.co.uk/courses/helicopter-stories-on-demand/

It's important to remember that the storyteller always chooses which character they will play in a story they have created. However, one of the key rules of Helicopter Stories is that children are NOT allowed to choose which of their friends take on the other roles and act on the stage alongside them.

Choosing our own role is vital. Where in life do we get to choose whether we will be a princess, a superhero or even a crying baby? But that is where choosing must stop. All other roles are cast randomly by taking turns around the stage, child by child. Each role is assigned based on where someone is sitting when that character is first mentioned in the story. One of the strengths of working in this way is that no one is left out. Every child has the opportunity to act in each other's stories and not just in the stories of their friends. They also have the right to say no, to decide they don't want to play, or that for this story they would rather watch. Working in this way, we give the children the autonomy to decide what works for them, but we also prevent a culture of exclusion developing where some children are excluded from joining in, in favour of those who are seen as more popular.

When Vivian Gussin Paley turned sixty, she became more and more aware of the voices in her classroom that proclaimed the words "you can't play." She struggled with the way children continually excluded each other from their games, or as she put it, *"How casually one child determines the fate of another."* Wanting to find a different way, she began to canvas the opinions of her kindergarten children and older children across the school, on how they would feel if there was a rule in her classroom that prohibited children from excluding another child in their play. The results of her conversations and this fascinating exploration of fairness can be found in her book *You Can't Say You Can't Play.*

Towards the end of the book, Vivian describes an unforeseen issue that arose when she finally decided to make *You Can't Say You Can't Play* a rule in her classroom.

> *"We are unprepared for a new issue that arises, one that confounds the teachers and disturbs the children… The classroom 'bill of rights' obviously does not cover story acting. The author owns all production rights. Though we have in theory at least rid ourselves of exclusivity in play, children can still reject one another when their stories are performed."*
>
> Vivian Gussin Paley - *You Can't Say You Can't Play*

Vivian talks to her children and discovers how painful it is for many of them when they are not chosen to act out in the stories of their peers. She immediately changes the way they do story acting and begins to cast the characters in turn from around the stage. Although a few children initially reject the idea, the results are incredible once this practice is in place. Girls take on boys' roles, boys take on girls' roles, and children who have never had a lead as a baddie, or a witch, end up getting cast in these significant parts and having more of a turn than they used to.

> *"Perhaps, in giving up control of who plays which character, the storytellers are liberating themselves from the demands of peer expectations."*
>
> Vivian Gussin Paley - *You Can't Say You Can't Play*

This new way of casting in Vivian's classroom sticks, and it will always be the way we deliver Helicopter Stories. However, some places still use the old way and allow children to cast all the roles themselves. I think some of them do this because they know no other way. Others do it for the same reason as Vivian: it is the storyteller's story, and there is a belief that as a result, they should be allowed to have whomever they want working on it. Interestingly, this is not the way of the professional world. The writer of a script rarely has a say in the casting or staging of their story. This is the role of the director, or a producer, or a casting agent. Films and theatre are collaborative processes, and each person involved adds their own unique part, building towards the final product.

So what is it like when children get to choose their own cast?

Several years ago, I visited a classroom where the storyteller was allowed to choose the actors. What I saw there convinced me that the only way to make Helicopter Stories a fair and safe activity for all children is to take it in turns around the stage, just like Vivian's children did after her research on exclusion. I will share with you my story and leave you to make up your own mind.

The school was in the USA. The kindergarten had been doing storytelling and story acting for several years, and I was keen to see how they did it. When all the stories had been scribed, the child whose story it was, stood by the teacher. She read out the characters, King, Princess, Dragon, Witch, and all the children who wanted to play each role put up their hands and squealed, "Me, me, me." The storyteller then had the opportunity to point to who they wanted to play each character. As I sat and watched, I found myself cringing.

One little boy, Billie, put his hand up every time. He was never chosen. The same happened in the following story and the next story. Billie did not get picked however quickly his hand shot up, or however much he pleaded. Five stories later and my heart was truly broken. Billie would have taken any role, but no one wanted him. Yet, some of the more popular children had a role in every story.

When the teacher had finished, I asked if I could demonstrate how I do Helicopter Stories. She kindly agreed. I used some stories I had brought with me, and the children took it in turn around the stage to act out these characters. By having a couple more trees than I needed, I made sure that Billie got the chance to play the monster. When it was his turn, he got onto the stage and acted being a monster as if his life depended on it. This was an Oscar-winning rendition. This was weeks and months of wanting to be on the stage and finally having his chance. Suddenly, the other children noticed and saw him in a new light.

After that, I scribed some stories and showed the children how we act out their stories using the same approach. The teacher was impressed, and the class decided that they would try using this new way of doing Helicopter Stories for one calendar month. After that, they would discuss if they wanted to stick with my way or go back to their old ways.

I returned to England. A couple of days after I got back, I received an email from the teacher. She told me about Billie. He was struggling to settle in kindergarten. He had no friends and was isolated from the group. But that day, when he played a monster, something changed, and the very next day, he got his first invitation to tea with another child. Billie was overjoyed, and as I read her letter, there were tears in my eyes. This is what it is all about; this is why it is so crucial that Helicopter Stories is fair and safe. Because when we work in this way, we get to see how other children play. How, rather than being closed off to the circle of friends we know, we get to see someone else's monster and to make friends with people we might never have played with. After the month was up, the children in Billie's classroom voted to keep acting their stories out in this way. The teacher said it had become safer, the children got to act in more stories and they stopped feeling excluded.

But there will always be some children, like Marta in the story above, who struggle with this rule. They desperately want their friends to be in their stories. If this happens in your classroom, the only advice I can give is to keep reiterating the rule and hold fast. Also, be wary. Children are ingenious at inventing ways to get around a rule that they don't like. I have heard children tell stories that go something like this.

"Chantal is the dragon, and the dragon saw Jamie, the dinosaur, and the dinosaur had another dinosaur friend, which is Martin."

During the scribing, it becomes obvious that the child is working out who will play which part and believes that if they put their classmate's name alongside the name of the character, they will get away with it. When this happens, I carry on scribing until the story is finished. I hate interrupting a child mid-story and breaking their flow. But when the story is finished, I put my pen down and say, "Do you remember that when we do Helicopter Stories, we don't get to choose who plays what character, so you know you said Chantal is the dragon, well when we get to that bit, it might not be Chantal's turn. If it isn't, then we will have to get someone else up to pretend to be Chantal pretending to be the dragon."

As the story is brought to life, the children around the stage find out that one of them is going to pretend to be Jamie pretending to be the dinosaur, and so on and so on. They very quickly realise that this ploy doesn't work. But be warned. I have seen a situation where the teacher didn't know what to do when this started happening in her classroom. She emailed me, saying she had led a session where when one child put the name of their friends in the story next to the various characters, she had allowed their choices to be honoured. The following week, in every story she scribed, the child did the same. She invited me in on an SOS, and it took quite a lot of work to restore the equilibrium and get the children to realise that this wouldn't work.

So, my biggest advice is to stick to this boundary. This is a rule that protects the children in your class. It stops them from being able to say to another, "I won't let you in my story if you do that." By working in this way, no child will feel excluded or never gets to have a turn. Also, having worked with the same class for three years, I have seen how much kinship can grow, and how trusting children are of each other when they have the opportunity to regularly play in each other's stories, and form a bond in this way. After all, that is what community is all about, and this simple rule can help us to exempt our classrooms from exclusion.

When you look at it like that, *It's Not Fair* becomes the fairest rule of all.